POET
MUSE

Sasha Nudél

THOUGHT
CATALOG
Books

THOUGHTCATALOG.COM

Published by Thought Catalog Books®, an imprint of Thought Catalog, a digital magazine owned and operated by The Thought & Expression Co. Inc., an independent media organization founded in 2010 and based in the United States of America. For stocking inquiries, contact stockists@shopcatalog.com.

Produced by Chris Lavergne and Noelle Beams
Designed by KJ Parish
Circulation management by Isidoros Karamitopoulos

thoughtcatalog.com | shopcatalog.com

First Limited Edition Print
Printed in the United States of America

ISBN 978-1-965820-20-9

POET MUSE

Dedicated to you, the poet and the muse,
creating and inspiring in equal measure.

Dear Reader,

Poet Muse is a collection born from the space where the poet and the muse blur into one. In these pages, you'll find poems from my first two collections, thoughtfully interwoven with new work. Each piece explores the mirror-like relationship we share with inspiration, showing how we reflect it, and how it reshapes us. *Poet Muse* opens the door to self-reflection and the quiet exploration of the questions we all carry but rarely speak aloud.

This isn't a book about perfect love. It's about raw, unfiltered emotion. It's about desire in its boldest, most honest forms. It's about claiming your voice, living fully, and daring to feel without apology.

You are not just a reader here. You are a poet. You are a muse.

May you find yourself in these lines, and perhaps leave with a few new ones of your own.

With gratitude,

Sasha

Pinterest Girl

Have you ever wandered through the
daydreams of a Pinterest girl,
where time stands still and old stories are never forgotten?
Soft moments of faded photographs
linger in a world of sentimental longing,
gently brushing your neck with a reminder.
Have you ever danced through a vintage dream?
Whispers from the past caress your ear,
drawing you in with warmth, familiarity,
and a wistful desire for what once was.
Have you ever been enchanted by nostalgia's tender pull,
as she calls to you from the corners of your soul,
where every breath you take
carries with it the weight of everything unsaid?
Nostalgia can be quite a seductress.

Take it From a Poet

I think everything in life is poetry.

Take it from a multi-passionate self-expressionist,

who marvels at the swirl in the foam of a morning matcha.

Take it from a hopeless romantic,

who gets lost in a reverie at the thought of a lover's touch.

Take it from a hopeful realist,

who romanticizes death,

for there is no better reminder to

indulge in the here and now.

Take it from an impractical dreamer,

who finds utopia in every profound connection.

Take it from a poet.

Curated Vulnerability

When did vulnerability become something we had to edit?
Aesthetic confessionals have become
a modern form of intimacy,
the grid, a digital altar
of how we want our fragility to be perceived.
A space where pain is stylized.
Lipstick smudged just enough to look like longing,
beautifully lit photos of a half-eaten croissant
next to a Sylvia Plath book,
tears filtered through VSCO presets
to make heartbreak look photogenic,
and captions that read like poems.
The coffee is cold by the time I finish arranging the scene.
We long to be seen,
but we fear being misunderstood.
So we share the version of our sadness that is easiest to love.
But deep down,
we hope someone sees through the curation,
past the filter and says:
"I know there's more. I want that too."

Awe

I went in search of meaning.
Awe arrived seeking a witness,
uninvited but deeply needed,
wanting nothing but my attention and stillness.
When the world stunned me silent
and burdened my path,
wonder softened the blow,
lifting me weightless with hope.
I stood ankle-deep at the brink of existence,
reality splitting in front of me like ripe fruit,
and vowed myself to awe,
to a soft undoing,
the still astonishment.

Bright Yellow

Somewhere between bright and dull,
between the sun and the earth,
content yet restless and insatiable,
my feet covered in dirt
yet hopelessly searching
for that bright yellow
to leave me blind in love again.

Meaningful Exchange

In the same way breath is not merely the inflation of lungs,

eroticism is not merely the friction of bodies.

It is not just desire,

it is witnessing,

a conversation whispered through flesh.

Who are you when you are naked,

not of clothes, but of defenses?

Who are you when you offer not just your body,

but your truth?

What secrets within you awaken

when another's eyes see you not as object,

but as answer?

To give oneself wholly to the moment,

to touch with consciousness,

to kiss with awe,

that is a meaningful energy exchange,

a vital life-force,

a thread between presence and sensation,

the blood-rush that reminds us

we are alive,

and infinite.

Untethered Sensuality

I was summoned by my Wild Feminine
to tend my fire with unruly softness,
untethered sensuality,
reckless creativity,
and compulsive playfulness.
I eagerly obliged.
When I engage with the world sensually,
through touch, taste, sound, and sight,
I become more attuned to the subtle beauty in the everyday,
transforming the mundane into
something rich with meaning.
I allow my senses to narrate and infuse ordinary events
with layers of significance and emotional depth.
I create a deeper connection to life's fleeting moments,
letting go of expectations and the weight of shoulds,
knowing in my heart that
you owe nothing to anyone,
and everything to time.

Wild Abandon

Touch me in earnest.
Purposeful and intentional,
strokes of grandeur
along my sternum.
Feel every thrum of my pulse,
every beat of my heart.
Stay there,
frozen in my words,
heated in my stare.
Plunge headlong into the pools of my collarbones.
Immerse yourself in my being, deep,
breath held, feelings exacerbated,
for I am yours
to make you feel
with wild abandon.

In Conversation with the Infinite

Why do I search for order in a universe
that does not ask to be understood?
Because I crave intimacy with it.
I yearn to feel that I am in conversation
with something greater than myself.
I'm made of longing,
silken, spiraling longing,
and she, my muse,
vast, silent, indifferent,
makes me want my words
to be more like her:
infinite and eternal.
I search for signs from her,
for connection, for pattern, for rhythm.
So I write,
to arrange the chaos of living.
I invent constellations in places
where others see only empty space.
I press my questions onto the
blank page of existence
and call it a love letter to the one
who taught me how to write in the dark.

Maybe

And maybe, just maybe,
the quiet glamour of 4:00 AM breakdowns
becomes a relic of a person no longer in your life.
And maybe, just maybe,
you use the journal not as therapy,
but as a sensual sanctuary,
where secrets are seduced into ink.
And maybe, just maybe,
you excavate emotions buried under the rubble
of what used to be,
just to remember how to love again.
And maybe, just maybe,
instead of calling it delusion or weakness,
you carry gratitude beneath your ribs
for the way your mind embellished the unbearable,
softened the jagged edges of pain,
spared your heart by rewriting reality
into something more poetic and palatable,
just to make the memory less sharp against your skin.

Playful Sentimentality

Hardheadedness failed me.

It will fail you too.

It will depreciate the value of your heart.

Instead, find that bud of sentimentality inside your chest

and allow it to open up into full bloom.

Get lost in the unleashed moments of life,

unstructured, free-flowing.

Grant free rein to your monumental imagination.

Be playful.

Play ignites creativity.

Creativity generates joy,

a natural high, so to speak.

This world desperately needs

a widespread flowering

of playful sentimentality.

The Only Religion

I have caught cruelty in the mouths of the righteous,

watched a childhood friend grow distant

after his grandmother told him

the name of my inherited faith,

so I can no longer pretend

to believe in the convenient rules

that are meant to save us

but so often suffocate.

If I am to believe in anything,

it is not in judgment,

but in the quiet, unrecorded acts of kindness.

In a world where temples are built

more for power than for peace,

I have found sanctuary in something

not constructed of bricks,

but of gesture.

Kindness, to me, is the purest form of devotion.

It doesn't ask me to kneel or confess.

It simply sees me.

It is the only religion that makes sense in my body.

When a stranger offers softness with no motive,

that is sacred.

So, if I am to be faithful to anything,

it must be to that.

Demons

The truth stands naked in the light, so I admit,

my vices and guilty pleasures both fuel

the demons I try so hard to outrun.

On the days when they catch me captive,

I rage against the chains that hold me,

but deep down inside I wonder

if I ever truly want to break free,

if I've somehow grown to need them.

What am I if I'm no longer touched by them?

If they vanish, will I still burn with feeling?

I want to offer my vulnerability

and see your own laid bare.

I'll hold it gently

and trust you'll stay,

no matter the weight,

for it is in our rawest moments

that we finally touch the deepest parts

of ourselves and each other.

Beneath the layers,

we're all just longing to be seen for who we are.

Quiescent Heart

Arouse me from the lethargy
of my set ways
by challenging my beliefs.
Prick me into consciousness
with a sharp and witty point.
Provoke a feeling
inside my quiescent heart,
and I promise
to make room for you in it.

Slow and Steady

A kiss that arrives not as an explosion,

but as a tide,

slow and steady.

To taste, not devour.

A connection that sets the eyes dancing before the skin.

It is not chaos.

It is sleeping in on a Sunday morning.

It is coffee waiting patiently to be shared

while we trace the shape of each other's thoughts.

There is a rare beauty in the unfolding,

one that asks for no haste,

a language built on patience,

a soul brushing against another,

not colliding but circling.

To learn the meaning of another's silences,

the story in a slight turn of a wrist,

the secret pulse at the neck

that steadies with trust.

A sanctuary with no fire alarms,

where time doesn't stop, but stretches.

Just a quiet warmth

that draws the body into softness,

barefoot and wide-eyed,

with the full awareness

that this will change you.

Nonverbal

In the parallel universe,

I'm brave enough to read my poems to your face.

Somehow, words feel limiting right now.

In this moment, they would diminish

what I truly wish to express.

What is it that I wish to express?

Cosmic connections are difficult things

to rationalize, aren't they.

Language often struggles to capture

the ineffable nature of deep emotional experiences.

My body seems to know the answers, though.

Do you speak body language?

Your hand is seeking an opening in my blouse,

a response to my question,

and I do not have the heart to protest.

Soul Ties

Not all love arrives loudly.
Some ties form like roots underground,
silent,
threading through stone and darkness
with the patience of meditation.
They reach, downward and inward,
they hold the earth together
the way love holds you upright
long after the storm has passed.
A soul tie is recognition,
as if they already know
the parts I've tried to bury,
as if we've met before
in dreams I forgot to write down.
Sometimes, the recognition is gentle.
Other times, it shakes you.
But it always leaves a mark.
A soul tie is knowing another's wildness
as intimately as your own
and calling it home.

Time-lapse

The world is crashing and burning,
self-destructing,
collapsing.
We're locking our eyes
in slow motion
while all that's around us
is time-lapsing.

Looped Affection

Trapped in a time-looped affection
(a blessing or a burden?),
where moments of connection replay again and again,
existing outside of linear time.
A timeless bond, immune to change or decay.
It blends comfort, nostalgia, and melancholy.
Suspended in a time-bent reality,
it's the only place the connection still lives,
expired and unresolved, yet eternalized.
A love that no longer exists in the present
but remains emotionally alive,
providing solace and pain in equal measure,
cyclical, with no need for resolution.
Sometimes, our deepest connections
are the ones we're meant to revisit forever.

Extraordinary

And I will always remember you

for the way your vibrant touch

rebelled against my dull routine

and turned ordinary into extra.

For the way your fingers

summoned goosebumps across my skin,

and your kisses gave rise to a cathartic release,

or what I like to call poetry.

Preserved in Pixels

Love now arrives dressed in filters and fleeting stories.

We fall for people we've never heard laugh,

seduced by curated chaos,

luminous, but fragile and elusive.

We chase each other's digital shadows,

yearning held hostage by distance,

whispers folded into captions;

each swipe, a secret caress,

each notification, a breath held.

Lovers become ghosts,

forever chasing the intimacy of a touch

that never quite lands.

We remain admirers preserved in pixels,

when all we crave

is a hand on our back, saying,

You're mine.

Inspire Me

Your love is never wasted,

for you once felt inspired by that person.

Lost moments, broken promises, quiet regrets transform me.

I clear the emotional debris,

moving through it, not around it,

uncovering hidden gems of inspiration.

I journey through the hurt with my journal as a companion,

filling lines with secrets of days long past.

And when words try me,

I open the pages that once carried the weight

of emotions so vivid and raw,

turn them into poetry,

and offer a smile of gratitude

for this intense surge of energy,

as if I've tapped into something larger,

more infinite than myself.

There's a sense of awe,

as if the universe whispered a secret just for me.

And I long more for the inspiration they brought

than the love they gave.

Rebellion

Life smiles at me,
like she is privy to something I am not.
"What are you thinking?" I ask.
She advises me to stop playing it safe,
and I eagerly oblige.
I erase the line between mad and courageous,
for they mean the same thing,
and proceed to engage in the ultimate
act of poetic rebellion:
living my life to the fullest.

Freedom

I once believed freedom was the art of direction,
the naming of every desire before it named me.
That if I could just control enough,
I might outrun the ache of not knowing.
What if it's not about the blueprint?
What if freedom lies in surrender,
in the widening of the soul?
What if it isn't about choosing the path,
but about learning to dance with the steps
the universe choreographs,
imperfect, unpredictable,
yet always meaningful?
I've found that when I no longer try to dictate the dance,
the steps come smoother.
They lead me not where I intended to go,
but where I was meant to feel
the soft synchrony of things
I never thought to ask for.
To let the universe lead,
even when its rhythm sways,
to trust that the missteps are music too,
not perfect, often off-beat,
but always present,
that feels like freedom to me.

Used For Art

I'm afraid I brought you here
under false pretenses.
But since you awakened my senses,
I figured using you for my art
is a pure intention.
So come here,
drop all your defenses.
Can you feel my heat
seeping into your flesh?
Breathe me in.
Love me senseless.
Maybe later,
we'll worry about the consequences.

The Psychedelic of Truth

Some flee to the jungle,
drink the bitter elixir
seeking revelations in the language of nausea,
hoping to burn their illusions in the fire.
They lie in the dirt
waiting for the cosmos to speak,
as if the horror of being oneself
could be cured by visions.
But I have found truth,
a more intrusive hallucinogenic,
more meticulous in its cruelty,
more liberating in its nakedness.
Unedited and unpretty,
it excavates me
until I'm nothing but breath and shadows.
When truth sits in my chest, clawing,
I speak it, sometimes,
as if I've mastered it,
because preaching is safer than practice.
And even if my voice shakes,
even if my body trembles,
it's still the most psychedelic thing I know.

No Threat

A moment in time cemented into my memory:
her robe falling open at the chest,
inviting fabric cascading in luxurious folds,
offering a preview
of what I already knew I couldn't live without;
a glimpse of what she menacingly called
a heart of stone.
But her warning posed no threat to my feelings.
Distance is too steep a price to pay
for the much-needed collapse of my ego.
The moments of euphoria
she weaved into my nervous system
are a generous gift
for being her brief abode of inspiration.
Our connection is self-evident.
To deny it would be in violation of fate.

Sculpture in a Museum

I have mastered the art of appearing untouched,
like a figure in a museum,
impenetrable, unreadable, unmoving,
a sculpture of composure.
My outward calm is a marble facade,
concealing the chaos of feeling
that churns beneath.
Only I hear the heartbeat
buried within the stone,
a mask that shields the ache of my tenderness.
I drape myself in a cape of detachment,
though my soul quivers beneath.
The more tender the spirit,
the more elaborate the defense.
The essence of me reveals itself only to those
who read between the lines,
buried beneath restraint.
To read me is to read haze,
a kind of softness that resists grasp,
but wraps itself around you,
if you let it.

Poetry

Sometimes, I am structure, rhyme, and reason.
Other times, I am free verse, confusion, and chaos.
I am poetry.

Exposed and Unseen

You see, sometimes
I withhold my feelings in writing
not because I want to be mysterious,
but because the truth,
when fully revealed,
shatters the calm I build around it.
So I write beside it.
I write almost.
I write nearly.
I leave the door open just enough.
I let the whitespace do the crying,
not out of restraint,
but out of self-preservation.
A line drawn just before the ache spills out.
The more I say, the more I give.
The more I give, the more I risk
being misunderstood.
And what a quiet violence that is,
to be exposed
and still unseen.

Pillows

Pillows, clouds stitched in stillness,
weightless vaults of bedtime whispers,
subconscious fantasies, conscious hopes.
Askew in the morning,
as if they too had wandered through dreams,
mirroring the disarray within.
They float beneath the weight of sleep,
cradling the chaos in my head tenderly,
as I toss and turn with questions
that outnumber the answers I have.
What is more real,
the waking world or the one I return to in dreams?
Are dreams echoes of other lives I've lived
or glimpses of ones yet to come?
Do I dream of who I am
or who I long to be?
Might death be nothing more
than slipping into a dream we never leave?
I better fluff my pillow.

Consumed Alive

I am an all-in kind of hopeless romantic,

for diluted love tastes like lukewarm cocoa to me.

I would rather burn my mouth

on the most flavorful feeling,

have it melt deeply into me

and consume me alive,

than dip my tongue into something unremarkable.

Truth Be Told

Truth, like love, is not safe.
When you speak your truth,
raw, unfiltered, unprotected,
your voice sounds hungrier,
as if it's been waiting
in the lining of your lungs for years
to suffocate the ego.
Truth shakes the scaffolding
of your polished self
and enters like a lover
in the middle of the night:
unannounced,
uninvited,
utterly necessary.
There's something beautiful in that risk,
because when you strip yourself
of the stories you told to stay loved,
what's left is *you*.
And in the ruins of illusion,
you find your voice again:
uncurated,
unapologetic,
alive.

Kinky

Life is kinky.
It bends you to its will,
rips you open,
caresses and feather-strokes you,
and then,
when you least expect it,
whips you.
It stings for some time, but then
pain works into discomfort
and discomfort into pleasure.
And suddenly,
you're alive
with more desire and more purpose.
Life is kinky.

The Trace I Leave

I am much more than a cemetery plot,
more than the absurd burden of stone,
cold, unyielding,
marking the place where flesh once resisted eternity.
The trace I leave will outlast marble.
It will live in the way someone glances at the ocean
and remembers desire,
in the way a kiss becomes a path,
in the heat between two hands
keeping the house warm through winter.
To exist only as a name in granite
is to surrender to finality,
and I have never accepted loss without revolt.

Color Palette

Mesmerized by the sky

reinventing itself daily.

From innocent bright blue,

to filthy gray,

to cold charcoal,

to morning's fairy-floss pink

with yellow undertones of melancholy.

From gloom to light,

what a talent.

Mesmerized by life's color palette.

Unsolicited

I never meant to fall into it,
but the universe,
mischievous in her understanding,
wrapped it neatly,
a pretty envelope,
wax-sealed with a capital L,
as if beauty could soften the intrusion.
(Clever of her,
knowing how easily I'm seduced by aesthetics.)
She sent it anyway.
Love arrived like mail meant for someone else:
half-open, torn at the edges,
stained with something that looked like ink,
or dirt,
or longing.
No return address.
No checkbox marked *"I didn't ask for this."*
And that's the thing about love,
it signs your name
long before you've given it
permission to stay.

E-love

Dance with me.

Even if it's virtual.

Don't you dare let ecstasy elude you.

Even if we're in different time zones.

Even if desire hasn't yet contracted the miles.

This tech-driven connection

casts a wire through outer space,

vast and uncharted,

much like the parts of me you awaken,

hidden, unspoken,

and yet to be fully discovered,

drawing you closer,

blurring into me,

exactly where you belong,

buried inside me.

The Match and the Struck

I have always mistrusted
the world's desire to divide,
the mind from the body,
thought from feeling,
man from woman.
But when the feminine,
fluid and radiant,
meets the masculine,
a force linear and driven,
it is not submission,
but a deep, complete,
harmonious expression.
The masculine brings focus;
the feminine offers the why.
She intuits, evokes.
He anchors, sets into motion.
Without her, he moves
but does not feel:
direction without dream.
Without him, she feels
but does not move:
alchemy without form.
They do not conquer each other.
Both the match and the struck.
They collide into a poem,
a soaring wholeness
alive with fire and flight.

Insatiable Thirst

The mere juxtaposition
of life and death
is so powerful,
it renders me incapable of anything
except trying to quench
the insatiable thirst
that being alive
has unearthed in me.

Open and Unafraid

So often I have stood on the precipice of affection,

paralyzed not by a lack of feeling

but by its sheer enormity,

the weight of it

unsettling everything I once believed was solid in me.

I build sanctuaries of solitude,

places where I can fold myself neatly.

I seek safety in every corner of my life

except in love.

Love is the one place I remain undone.

Unfolded.

Unhidden.

And so, I leap.

Even if my knees quiver.

Even if silence is the only hand holding mine.

Because numbness is its own kind of disappearance,

not loud, not violent,

just a slow erosion of what makes me human.

Safety offers stillness,

but love wakes me.

So I choose to feel,

recklessly,

without apology,

open and unafraid.

Masterpiece

I once stumbled upon a striking piece of art.

His grandiosity could feel intimidating.

A handsome glass mosaic

inlaid with small, colored fragments

of his past and present,

seducing my senses.

True to its definition,

the art invoked a reaction

by disrupting my inner peace.

Awakened and intrigued, I looked closer.

I studied him,

every crack, scratch,

and all the plaster holding his pieces together.

Infatuated with the masterpiece,

I let him consume me.

Until one day, I looked too close

and saw right through him.

The newly-discovered truths

exploded in a mass of fiery shards

and bit into my chest.

Pain ripped through me so fast,

it took my heart rate from steady to wild in a single beat.

In that clarifying moment

I realized that art is not meant to be intellectualized,

but rather, reveled in.

Velvet Fever

I romanticize everything.
It's a sickness of softness,
a velvet fever.
A glance becomes a vow,
a laugh becomes a hand on my bare shoulder,
witty comeback, a love profession.
Awash in the weight of the mundane,
reality rarely blushes,
stiff and literal,
but I keep flirting,
I keep undressing for a moment
that never asked to be special.
I don't wait for meaning,
I make it.
I don't fall in love.
I create it.

Now

The word *now* is so invigorating.

A razor-sharp gust of wind

rushing me to live in the moment.

The word *now* is so hypnotic.

It gives wings to my imagination

and watches it drift beyond thought.

The word *now* is so provocative.

It demands I feel,

and make others feel too.

Theatrics

We clink glasses in a room full of borrowed smiles,

but none of them ever brush the skin of our loneliness.

I sit among them, nodding, laughing,

suffocated by the theatrics of politeness,

while my real self starves beneath the surface.

Our gestures are rehearsed,

our warmth, staged,

and still we wonder

why no one feels real anymore.

We perform ourselves for each other,

wearing masks that never dare

to know the wild,

unkempt truth of the soul.

Even the light feels choreographed,

dancing across our civilized detachment.

All this beauty,

and not one soul dares to bleed.

And so we vanish, gracefully,

never touched,

never truly seen.

Love Worn Thin

Too much ego will turn a lover into a leaver.

No, I didn't fall out of love.

It was more severe.

A loss of trust in someone I once viewed

through the lens of idealism.

Disenchantment replaced admiration.

Feeling collapsed into thinking.

Reality washed over me

and left me in a whirlpool of conflicting emotions

competing for dominance:

Feed his ego or feed my soul?

Does he care for my heart,

or am I just a reflection of his desire?

Does he love me

or does he simply need my applause?

A love worn thin cleared away all doubt.

I'll see myself out.

Substance

Be picky about the human substance
you allow into your mind and body.
It can be a vitamin,
a pain reliever,
or slow-acting poison.

Read Me Like You Mean It

I wonder if you feel it,
that faint pulse between the sentences,
that tremor in the spine of the book.
The truest lines are always invisible:
unwritten entries inside me,
revealed in sighs, in glances, in silence.
This book is not a confession.
It's a seduction.
Every sentence is a stocking
rolled slowly down my thigh.
Can you hear the gasp between stanzas?
The wet breath of a run-on thought?
Read me aloud,
as if I were a sacred text
unearthed from beneath silk sheets.
Can you taste the eroticism of vulnerability?
To read my secret thoughts
is to touch me
in the most sensitive places.
You can underline my softness with ink,
highlight my pleasure in yellow,
and when you close this book,
you'll still feel me on your fingertips.
Pass it on,
so they can feel me too.

Protect

He said,

"I'll protect you from all of your vividly painful dreams.

And when I hear your soul scream,

I'll keep it gently cradled

to protect you from egos overinflated.

When empty words are thrown your way

and cause you pain,

I'll be your numbing novocaine.

I'll protect you from mannequin souls,

from villains and trolls,

from the remnants of your emotional past.

I'll even protect you from time flying too fast.

From insecurities and all of your vices,

I'll remind you that perfection is lifeless."

He concluded,

"To the love of my life,

while simultaneously found and lost,

I'm afraid,

I need to protect you from me the most."

A Friend Like a Galaxy

When my 9 year-old asks how many friends I have,

I pause, caught in the stillness

between truth and performance.

There is only one.

The one who listens when I speak in unfinished sentences,

who hears the silence beneath my words.

The one who doesn't feel the need

to smooth my edges to make me easier to carry.

Instead, she cradles the sharpness.

The one who lets me show up unwashed, unraveling,

and still doesn't pull away.

The one who sees me in the questions

I don't know how to ask,

in the pauses I can't explain,

in the versions of myself

that feel too much for anyone else.

And when we disagree,

it is not a fracture but an invitation

to whisper stories of different landscapes,

then fold back into the unison of us.

So when my child asks again,

I'll say it simply:

"Only one. But that one feels like a galaxy."

Jugular

Nature roars, ground shakes.
Here comes my internal earthquake.
Love throbs dangerously in my jugular vein.
Are you my safe haven or life-threatening pain?
The gentle vulgarity of our touch,
and there is no such thing as too much,
when in one destined motion
two rivers flow into one ocean.

Naked Truth

What a holy place to stand,

naked in one's truth,

untranslatable,

and still whole.

There is no freedom in being seen

only in fragments,

edited to fit someone else's comfort.

I've learned that truth

does not always hold hands with belonging.

Sometimes, it builds distance,

low, quiet, irreversible.

Still, I choose to be misunderstood

rather than adored for something I'm not.

Because what use is love,

if it asks me to disappear

in order to keep it?

Doppelgangers

I most enjoy being in touch with what makes us animals.

Not time management,

social pressures,

work-life, or due balances.

I most enjoy the visceral feeling of desiring,

as if we've encountered one another in the wild.

Will I take or be taken?

Fully. Nakedly.

Unrestrainedly.

Will I satiate my own hunger

or be eaten alive?

Animalistically, yet humanely.

Much like in love, in the wild,

resilience and courage are essential for survival.

Much like in love, pain is an inherent part

of the profound connections we seek as animals.

Wild is just the alter ego of love.

It's felt in the marrow of bones,

when we risk ourselves in vulnerability and uncertainty.

I most enjoy surrendering to my primal instincts,

so my imprint is felt as vigorously and as menacingly,

as the breaking of bones in the animal kingdom,

where love and risk are doppelgangers.

Abundance

Fall.

Fall hard.

Fall boldly.

Fall shamelessly.

Fall harder than the guard you are putting up.

Fall to crack yourself open

and show the abundance of love you carry inside.

Because you do.

We all do.

Fall.

Where the Poem Begins

I write poems that I want to feel in my body,
not in my brain,
words that throb beneath the skin
like a shiver, a heartbeat,
a breath held too long.
I want the words to move through me
the way music does,
to resonate in my bones,
to make my heart shift rhythm.
I am here chasing sensation:
the hunger before heat,
the tremor before tears,
the ache before desire.
I do not write to embellish,
I write to expose the nerve,
to awaken the skin,
to pierce the surface of memory
just behind my ribs.
When the words sting a little,
warm,
haunt,
that is where the poem begins.

From Lust to Death

Dear Death,
I wonder,
do you ever wish you could feel
what I feel
when I press against a soul?
We keep finding each other
in the mouths of the same lovers.
You, stealing their breath.
Me, giving it back
in gasps and moans.
I know you feel me
in the tremor
just before they close their eyes.
We both leave them undone.
You come when the candle burns out.

I come when the wax begins to drip.

Your touch is forever.

Mine is fever.

We both love the ruin,

dress it in poetry,

call it romance.

Tell me,

have you ever been kissed

like you were the last sin

worth committing?

I think I'd like to be your first.

Almost yours,

Lust

Jaded

Can we linger in the infatuation phase a little longer?

Before time brings our flaws to light.

Before we regret our confessions.

Before the threads that bind us begin to fray.

Before I become jaded, and you, heartbroken.

Hurry.

Pour yourself onto me like honey.

Against better judgment.

Mold into the crevices of my soul.

A meaningful bond, albeit short-lived.

And please,

do that thing I love the most,

where you grip my throat like a vice and kiss it.

Hurry.

Before the sun burns itself out.

French Kiss

In my amorous
pursuit of happiness,
I lock lips with life,
its good,
its bad,
its messiness.
Too much passion in me
for a friend zone.
I'm French kissing it.
Yes. Tongue and all.

Prayer And Profane

I have become a voyeur
to my own undoing.
My gaze on myself
as his mouth moves lower
is its own intoxication.
There is only the pleasure
of slipping beyond
the borders of control,
letting the body rebel
against the mind.
We speak of sin,
but I have tasted the sacred
in the slow swell
beneath his touch,
in the way he shivers
before entering me.
And I watch
as I become both prayer and profane,
seduced by the power of surrender.
I do not want salvation.
I want to be ruined
with worship.

De-armor

I willingly lend my being
to the thrall of pain, melancholy, and nostalgia,
because I am convinced
the only way to achieve emotional sturdiness
is by making space for vulnerability.
What used to be rigid armor across my chest
is now a delicate blouse offering a tender embrace.
It turns out, the armor I wore all my life
was only useless scrap metal.
Had I not realized sooner,
it might have blocked my life force
from flowing freely through my body,
might have stifled my potential,
might have stalled my creativity.
The porous fabric of my new blouse
lets me breathe fully and openly,
free from the counterproductive
physical and emotional blockages.
My openness is my protection.

Stolen Lines

I wish to write about the sun,

the moon,

and the star-lit sky,

but you keep stealing my poems.

With you hiding between my lines,

I forget what it feels like

to be clear-headed.

Lively Lifelessness

We live a lively lifelessness,
where the surface is animated,
but beneath it,
there's a void,
a hollow silence,
where passion, purpose, and connection
ought to reside.
The challenge lies in moving toward a life
that is vibrant
and truly alive from within.
May we awaken to a living
that is both embodied and meaningful
by tending to the quiet sparks within,
by honoring what stirs the soul,
and by choosing, again and again,
to live from the inside out.

Head in the Clouds

Longing lingers around me like mist,

unseen, but ever-present.

Judgment for indecent exposure,

for laying my soul bare,

revealing my vulnerabilities,

unmasking my naked truths

does not faze me.

Historically, such trials have only ignited

the artist's vision

and sparked the poet's dreams.

Often, having your head in the clouds

is more productive

than keeping your feet too firmly planted.

For in the sky, bathed in sunlight,

there are no limits,

only infinite paths.

Cynics

Two cynics don't cancel each other out.
So for the time being,
let's pretend we're both honest
and hopelessly romantic.

A Cage for the Soul

I was handed superstitions
like heirlooms, well-intentioned,
cloaked in the garments of love and tradition,
but they served only to bind me
to narratives that were not my own.
For what is superstition,
if not the echo of someone else's fear?
And what is fear, if not a cage for the soul?
These rules were sewn into the lining of my being,
seemingly harmless, even poetic,
rituals of belonging.
But over time, they became shadows in my mind,
hesitation, guilt, and fear,
where there should have been light.
I was trained not to tempt fate,
and in doing so,
I ceased to tempt life.
To strip myself of inherited illusions,
to burn away what was never truly mine
was my sacred act of reclamation,
and I became the author of my own becoming.

No Touching

We made love.
Clothes on. No touching.
Caressing each other's dreams,
tickling goals,
nibbling aspirations,
dirty-talking about our fears,
massaging inspiration,
fingering secrets,
licking the mind's filthiest corners,
swallowing insecurities,
devouring heartbreaks,
toying with feelings,
laving emotional aches,
stroking egos,
satiating yearnings,
satisfying desire that's burning.
We made love.
Clothes on. No touching.

No More

Somewhere between *meant to be*
and *we are no more*.
Somewhat blessed
and doomed at the same time.
Sort of at peace,
but also at war,
now that I'm still yours,
and you're no longer mine.

The Kiss

The kiss arrived
not like a gentle greeting,
but a violent return,
a rupture in time
that shattered the quiet of my skin.
No longer just a meeting of lips,
I felt it in my chest,
the collision of histories,
desires,
silences.
What was flesh
became feeling.
What was warmth
became knowing.
There was no language,
only a shift,
almost imperceptible,
like gravity deciding
to lean a little harder,
and in that,
a thousand poems.

The Way You Say Mine

The way you whisper *mine*
isn't a claim but a calling,
like you're naming something sacred
that always belonged to you,
like a secret you're honored to keep.
Mine, said like a prayer
muttered against skin instead of sky.
Worship, not possession.
You say *mine,*
and something inside me softens
instead of bracing.
There's a violence in how gently you want me,
and I let it ruin me with reverence.

Borrowed Time

Exchanging big words frivolously,
knowing we're on borrowed time.
Seriously,
if you're still caging your love rigidly,
do you mind bending its definition, possibly?
How can you not fall for people constantly?
And if you do,
let them know immediately,
before death hits and runs, drunkenly.

Desire

Is desire a compass or a labyrinth?
I follow it, devotedly,
and it always leads me
to another version of myself,
reveals another hidden facet.
Desire is poetic.
It's existential.
Burning, urgent, intoxicating.
It's not a guide, it's a spiral,
and I let it carry me
not toward a destination,
but deeper into becoming.
In chasing it, I meet myself,
not once, but endlessly,
each time more true than the last.
Desire gives, and it consumes.
To follow it is to burn,
until I am echo and ash,
scattered,
and still wanting.

Life

Life.

I am not in it just for a voyeur's delight.

This hearty appetite

is meant to taste every corner of every emotion,

to dive deep into a bottomless ocean,

to partake in a grand love story

of which I am the prime suspect,

to experience love,

as thrilling as an unidentified flying object.

I am in it to create a rapid-fire montage

of all the striking moments,

but commit only the best ones to memory:

of egos breaking, souls colliding,

getting lost in perpetual reverie.

Feverish Creatures of Youth

One day,

I'll wake up in a body that no longer fits

the way I remember myself.

My skin will hold the ruthlessness of time,

my hands, once radiating light,

will move more slowly,

more purposefully,

as if every gesture now carries weight.

And they,

the beautiful and unknowing,

feverish creatures of youth,

will look at me with eyes

that cannot fathom I was once like them,

as if I never spoke truths

before I understood their consequences,

made wild mistakes in the name of desire,

kissed without caution,

or cried over the kind of love

that leaves you hollow and holy all at once.

And maybe I won't tell them.

Maybe I'll just smile,

like I don't still write poems

about the ghost of who I used to be.

But I'll remember her.

I'll always remember her.

Sienna

I knew her name
before I knew I wanted to have a child.
Sienna.
Like the name of a flower I had not yet seen
but somehow remembered.
She arrived softly,
a gentle pollen swirling beneath my ribs.
All the world paused, tilting slightly,
to make room.
She is everything I ever wanted and more,
the more I never thought to ask for.
My daughter is old soul and newborn wonder,
eyes full of quiet moons and deep questions.
When I mention getting older,
she folds into silence,
because to her
time is a tally of days
not gained but counted down.
And I stand helpless at the edge of that knowing.
Every moment,
I feel her heartbeat in my throat,
I watch the most breakable part of me
learning to fly.
Every day, I hold her
and I hope this world is gentle
with something so luminous, so electric, so wild.

Wishful Apology

Hey, you. Yes, you, my midnight madness,

my morning ache, my daily sadness.

Although a hundred lies too late I am,

I'll try with everything I can

to show the deep regret I now live with,

the nagging scar inside my soul,

and I'd give everything I own

to reincarnate you in my arms.

I'm sorry to have caused you harm.

Now, until the very end of time,

to alleviate this pain of mine,

all I can do is punch walls,

throw fists and scream

over the pain I've put you through

and for destroying my own dream

of dancing for eons upon this earth with you.

Ode to the Wild

I, too, have cradled sorrow like a second skin.

But I was not made to be a chronicler of agony.

I was made to be a lover of life,

a celebrant of complexity,

a mirror to every unspoken desire.

I believe in fire,

not just the kind that burns,

but the kind that illuminates.

That soft, golden heat of presence,

of passion,

of poetry.

We are not meant to live half-alive,

suspended in the wound.

Life, in all its unbearable beauty

demands that we burn

in the blaze of becoming ourselves.

Let others name their ghosts.

I will write odes to the light,

to the yearning,

to the wild.

Beneath the Mask

The smile, a fragile mask
woven from hope and desperation,
hides a war no one sees.
Each laugh a truce,
a quiet pause between battles,
a delicate ceasefire
between what we show and what we bury.
Maybe we learn to hold space
for what remains unspoken.
Maybe we acknowledge that beneath the surface,
everyone carries something
worth understanding.

Blink

I love it when the sky makes me feel insignificant.
The daily changes in its color are emblematic
of how temperamental life is.
All we have to do is accept the mood swings.
How would you know to appreciate the blueness
if you'd never seen the blackness to compare it to?
Blink, darkness.
Blink, brightness.
Blink, chaos.
Blink, blank slate.
Blink, worries.
Blink, peace.
Blink, the vast nothingness of every day
to make something glorious out of.

Mama, Papa

They crossed oceans,
not just of water,
but of loss unspoken,
of pain carried like a second skin.
My parents wore grief like a shadow,
always behind them,
always touching the edges of their joy.
My mother walked through the ashes of her own family
while still learning how to be a daughter.
My father, whose childhood offered no emotional shelter,
still built one for me
from what little he had.
Sometimes, I feel my own sorrow rising,
but I dare not call it suffering.
I know the story before mine.
I know the silence they held
like a second language.
And so, I carry my life
with a quiet gratitude,
delicately,
like a glass vessel,
always aware of the hands
that passed it to me,
trembling but unbroken.

The Rare Ones

I have built an altar for intimacy,

lit candles for connection,

written poems in the language of longing,

but the truth is

I find most people unbearable.

I wander the world disappointed,

impatient,

disenchanted,

yet still, I look for someone

whose presence splits me open in recognition.

I crave the rare ones

who make the room feel less like a cage,

who bleed when they love.

It is the loneliest ache to

need connection like air

but find most people impossible

to breathe around.

And so I remain

suspended in the waiting,

too alive for the surface,

too delicate for the depths

where no one dares to follow,

to stumble upon the clear-eyed,

the unrestrained,

the unflinching.

Memento Mori

The fire in my belly comes roaring to life,
surpassing the boundaries of skin and bone,
erupting onto the pages of my journal.
I have no business experiencing writer's block,
for I am a conduit for the universe and its magic.
I am here to live in and write of
a state of poetic arousal.
I am here to defy mortality
with levity and contagious vitality.
Remember, you must die.
But death only feels bleak
if you overlook its deeper meaning.

Not Afraid to Die

When you know the fabric of time is thin.

When you realize the root of *sin*cere is sin.

When you fail to find the good in *good*bye.

When you learn you've been fed a lie.

When the heartbreak makes your ribs crackle.

When saving broken glass becomes a losing battle.

When the pit in your stomach is no

longer a butterfly flutter.

When your daydreams are now just hurtful mind clutter.

When pain camouflages itself in your smile,

I start to understand why.

Why so many people

are not afraid to die.

Inked Expressions

I write to reconnect with myself,
each word an arrow
leading me out of the labyrinth
of my own making,
built from the roles others wrote for me.
The page does not ask for explanations,
nor does it judge.
It simply receives.
All the contradiction, sentiment,
and violence within me.
I pour, I confess, I unravel,
and the page patiently accepts me,
word for word.
There's something to be said
for how ink can soothe more than talking,
how self-expression heals in ways
words alone often fail to.

Rebellious Desire

I choose to write about passion,

not because I am blind to suffering,

but because I see no virtue in worshipping it.

They want me to speak of wounds,

to narrate my pain

as if it were a moral obligation.

But I believe in the alchemy of longing,

in the intoxication of being alive.

Desire is my rebellion.

Lust, my resurrection,

a portal to connection, ecstasy, expansion.

And life itself,

what is it, if not an aching,

persistent seduction?

Femme Fatale

The myth of the eternal femme fatale
is that time strips her of her allure,
but time only smooths the edges,
making her magic more potent,
thicker on the tongue.
Her power lies not in the curve of her hip,
nor in the gleam of youth in her eye,
but in the depth of self-knowledge,
her devastating grace,
an eroticism that is intellectual, poetic,
wholly self-possessed.
She grows quieter in her presence,
more surgical in her silences.
Her seduction is no longer just
in the softness of her skin,
but in the sharpness of her gaze,
lighting candles in the dim corridors of herself.
She no longer plays the role,
she authors it.
And isn't that the ultimate seduction?
To linger in the mind not through presence,
but in the exquisite tension
of all things unsaid,
yet indelibly felt.

Reminder

Time is palpable.

It pulsates inside me like a vital organ.

A simultaneously fragile and omnipotent

clicking reminder

to stare at the sunset a little longer,

indulge in the company of my favorite people a little deeper,

luxuriate in togetherness with a lover more vulnerably,

and plunge into this journey of life

headlong.

Tick.

Tock.

Perfect Rhyme

There go her demons,

so masterfully disguised in the grin,

on her skin,

and the essence within

seducing me once more.

You would think that shiver down in my core

and the sirens going off in my veins

would remind me of the pain,

of the time she split my life into

'unremarkable' and 'amused to have finally found a muse.'

But when her wild enveloped my mind,

and grew roots around my spine,

I realized that she and I

are a perfect rhyme.

Love That Gives

There's a quiet, exquisite heartbreak
in letting go of the need
to be the source of someone's joy.
Soft and brutal at once.
Drenched in longing,
beautiful in its sadness.
I want your pleasure,
even if it doesn't come through me.
To place another's happiness
above your own desire or pride,
a love that asks for nothing in return.
It is simply offered.
The language of a soul stripped bare,
the voice of a lover
who has transcended ego.
And yet, I wonder:
is this surrender a liberation
or the quiet death of self?

Defying Time

If you were to ask me
what Bukowski and I have in common,
it must be the trauma
of knowing how fragile and short,
off and on, full of hurt,
this life is.
But with absolute clarity,
an open mind,
and a healthy dose of vulgarity,
both Bukowski and I
could assert, through perfect rhyme,
that to overlove
is to defy time.

Destructive Muse

Muse. A lover.

A brutal, intoxicating, and overwhelming force.

She reflects the parts of the poet

that fuel creation by risking his existential collapse.

He writes his best work while emotionally unraveling

under the weight of her punishing beauty.

Calmness doesn't move him.

Only chaos.

Like when the ocean thrashes and the wind howls,

yet you still feel magnetically drawn to deep waters,

pulled in by their unapologetic, volatile energy.

She is the catalyst for his genius,

the source of salt-worn metaphors

from letters tossed into the ocean,

the rip current that intensifies his poetic punch.

He swims toward her, reckless with courage,

knowing that to feel deeply

is to go under gracefully.

Incoherent

Losing control of my faculties,

as your lips swallow my laugh,

your kisses muffle my moans,

and an unintelligible *I love you*

escapes my mouth

through all the incoherent thoughts.

Is that what being drunk in love feels like?

Maybe It Will Bloom

There is comfort in the ritual of falling apart,

the slow, aesthetic art

of self-destruction

dressed in romance.

We make relics of our sorrow

so the ache sounds beautiful,

because meaning,

even when mythologized,

hurts less than emptiness.

And even in unraveling,

there's a flickering promise,

that something new, something truer

will take root in the ruins.

And this time,

maybe, it will bloom.

Equilibrium Unsettled

His soft soul and rough hands.

Her soft hands and rough soul.

He grabs love with a claim.

Her energy is fierce and unyielding.

He tries to anchor himself,

but she is wild, unpredictable, drawing him in deeper,

until they both forget how to balance.

His equilibrium unsettled by her intensity.

She is stumbling, regret-free.

The steady pulse of his calm is shaken by her fire,

a heat that consumes yet ignites,

flames dancing in the quiet spaces

between their perfect silence.

They lose and find their serenity

inside the rippled bedsheets.

Risk It All

Like stepping into quicksand,

an all-consuming grip of yours,

fingers interlaced, palms kissing, desires fused,

sparks a flare-up of possessiveness.

I relish watching your impulse to risk it all

seize you the moment your fingers connect with my skin.

The taste of my moans in your mouth

unearths an oceanic yearning for all the possibilities.

I, too, will risk it all

for this unparalleled feeling of carefree

that we envelop each other in.

Embracing, Not Becoming

There comes a time in the journey of the self,

when one must reject the role of the mourner.

Not because pain ceases to exist,

but because one has learned

to embrace it without becoming it.

Where Shadows Forget

My legs tighten around your waist,

not to hold, but to merge,

pulling you deeper

into the gravity of this moment.

"Stay," I whisper.

"Right here,

where we blur,

where every part of me

answers without question,

and everything I am

leans quietly into you,

until even our shadows

forget which body casts them."

Sensible Love

Is there a sensible way to love?

A way to calculate and weigh up

all cons and pros,

to predict and avoid any loss,

to chart love's trajectory

and approach your decision objectively?

The problem is,

there isn't a scale to weigh

the giddy release in my tummy,

his encyclopedic knowledge of my body,

the effortless conversation shared between two,

the laughter leaving my ribs sore.

Even the post-breakup agony.

Yes, it hurts, but please give me more.

The answer is 'no.'

Sensible love is an oxymoron.

I want it to feel counterintuitive. Different. Foreign.

I want no part of my soul left untouched,

each mouth's corner left upturned.

The only sensible way to love

is the one where you're willing and eager to get burned.

Every Lifetime

I am convinced
we have touched each other
in every lifetime.
It must be the way
my body trembles in recognition,
hands stutter in motion,
and the sound of my heartbeat
reverberates across every frequency
that proves me right.

Outrageous Lovers

I want love that doesn't flinch
when I unravel.
Imagine the magic
of coming back to yourself
by walking toward someone else.
What a tender, wild thing it is
to be wanted exactly as we are.
When the universe folds itself small,
and it is only him
and the breath between us,
when the daily inertia of life buries
who we really want to be,
what we really long to do,
and still, time bends
to make room for lovers like us.
To live as outrageous lovers,
that is the quiet rebellion,
to drop our masks
in the middle of laughter
and call it love.

Wild Animals

Having touched you once,
the wild animals
inside my cells
released chemicals
and they rebelled
against the skepticism
that's overtaken my heart.
My love,
I tamed those wild animals,
and those excruciating memories
are now my worst enemies,
for they are haunting my reveries
while you and I are apart.
I'll fight for you for months, years, and centuries.
Your arms, your eyes, your lips are my remedies
against the trivial pleasantries.
You're all the beautiful melodies,
and one of life's biggest tragedies is
that mine you are not.

Some Hands

There are fingerprints on my ribs
where you held me open.
I sought intimacy without grandeur,
closeness without pretense,
a poised hunger for something real,
stripped of ego and theatrics.
You sought openness without armor,
my soul stripped bare beneath your gaze,
but only so you'd know where to strike.
Vulnerability is a gift,
but dangerous in the wrong hands.
And I gave it anyway.
There is no shame
in the way we unravel for someone,
no shame in softness mistaken for surrender.
But some hands only reach for what's open,
so they can see how it breaks.

Bright Eyes

In the impatience of bated breath.
In the vibrancy of rosy lips.
In his lightness and great depth.
In the significance of his fingertips.
In the playfulness of his voice.
In the urgency to make plans.
In his carefree nature of choice,
and the mightiness of his hands.
Under the curtains of my own eyelashes.
In the stare of his bright eyes.
In the deepening of all six senses
is where my desire lies.

Listening

I would not be a poet

if I did not possess the gift of listening,

not merely to words,

but to what trembles beneath them.

I've written books

out of the things people don't mean to say:

the nervous laugh, the hesitations,

the accidental confessions,

the silence after a name.

It is in these subtle betrayals of the self

that the truth reveals itself,

and I press them like wildflowers

between the pages,

to keep what was once alive.

Your Heart Is a Fist

At the risk of sounding trite,

allow me to remind

that your heart's primary function is to contract.

In fact, after contraction,

it will expand.

and since you are in command

of your attitudes, your reactions

to various turns of events,

planned and unplanned,

your heart is both spacious and grand,

built to acknowledge, sit with, and process

all that you feel.

Be it love too damn surreal,

profound intimacy, nagging heartache,

or inexplicable bliss.

Your heart is a mighty fist.

The one that will punch against what doesn't seem right.

And other times, clenched snug and tight,

it will embrace and hold onto

whatever makes the lighthearted feel light.

Thought-less

Sometimes, I leave the window open
just to hear the world exist without me.
I only wish to hear something
that isn't my own ceaseless mind-chatter
echoing off the walls.
The moon, like a good friend,
privy to all my secrets,
spills herself across my floor,
as if she's showing up just for me.
I light a candle like it's a wish,
pretend the flicker is a heartbeat.
We meditate through the noise,
the moon and I,
admiring the smoke,
delicate, shapeless, constantly transforming,
gone before a thought could settle.
Before I know it,
the morning clouds,
slow-moving, ever-shifting,
like thoughts that pass without clinging,
uncover the sun,
offering a bowl of morning light.
And I drink it slowly.

Loneliness

People speak of loneliness,

a feeling so unfamiliar to me.

How can I feel lonely when every day

the sky embraces me,

the earth caresses my feet,

the sun plants warm tender kisses on my forehead,

the air fills my lungs with inspiration,

the ocean dedicates poems to me?

I am never alone.

Anchored

Solitude used to feel like being wrapped in cashmere

and still shivering.

Now, it feels like a warm cup of tea

I don't have to rush.

I get to take long walks

without needing to be found.

I let silence stretch its legs,

eager to hear what it might say.

I'm not alone.

I'm just alone right now.

And that's the difference love makes:

solitude becomes something you choose,

not something you survive.

You are the reason

I get to lose myself in a daydream

without fear.

Because somewhere,

around the bend of time and space,

you're waiting.

The anchor.

The safe return.

Unrepentant

I don't write to be read.
I write to be felt,
like a shiver down your spine you weren't expecting.
I like my words feral and unrepentant,
not meant to rhyme, but to rupture.
A knife hidden under my tongue.
Call it poetry if you want,
but I'm just chasing words sharp enough
to undress the parts of you
you forgot were naked.

Failures

Like training wheels or rough drafts,

mistakes guide you

toward your true calling,

pulling you from blind assurance

into quiet self-awareness.

You learn what you're meant for

by seeing what you're not.

You find answers to questions

long abandoned:

what drains you,

and what excites you,

where you falter,

and where you fly,

what you resist,

and what you embrace,

what quiets you,

and what awakens you.

Failures were invented

so you could find your purpose.

Rib Spreader

The universe only speaks to the open-hearted ones,

those who haven't lost their imaginativeness or hope,

despite the world-weariness.

Those who remain rich in soul and compassion,

as the daily assault of the mundane wears them down.

So, clamp onto the center of your sternum,

spread your ribs apart,

and allow your most vital self

to connect with the greater universe.

Your mission, should you choose to accept it,

is to tantalize, tease, and mentally stimulate yourself,

until you live in an ongoing state of poetic arousal.

Self-Intimacy

Two spritzes of my favorite perfume,

citrusy with a green-musky twist,

that feels both clean and intriguingly complex, like me,

misted with love and attention onto my cozy robe,

a velvety embrace.

The first sip of coffee in the morning

(a love letter to myself, my own company),

slowly brewing me back to life,

not rushed, not distracted,

just me waking softly

and choosing myself before the noise of the day.

Cultivating the kind of romance,

where I am both lover and beloved.

Solitude, a secret affair with myself,

silence not as emptiness,

but as presence,

defying the idea that intimacy

requires another body in the room.

Courage

I have a life-long muse and she is wild and courageous.

She teaches me to be open-minded,

empathetic, and creatively outrageous.

She pushes me to look at the world

through another person's perspective,

humbles me and reminds me to be self-reflective.

She once inspired me to dismantle society's firmly held,

unreasonably imposed beliefs

when I was feeling discouraged.

And that was when I learned

that curiosity begets courage.

Curiosity is my muse's name.

Her unapologetic audacity

is what I aspire to exude and exemplify.

And the most prized lesson she ever taught me was that

for those without courage, magic is hard to come by.

Enough

My bones know the weight of now.
But my thoughts drift like petals on water,
untethered and wistful,
beautiful but rootless.
I yearn to live where my feet touch the earth,
to inhabit what is already mine:
this present moment.
Instead, I am always almost here.
And then a thought insists on being heard,
and the world resumes its ticking,
and traffic hums like a promise,
and the inbox fills itself again,
and then the minutes pull me forward,
and then,
and then,
and then.
I draw a deep breath in.
I ask the day to loosen its grip.
Breathe out.
I come home to this body.
I anchor myself in the now,
unhurried, undemanding,
enough.

Anew

If I had a chance to create the world anew,
what would I do?
I would start with myself.
I would dive into every connection
with sheer, unbridled expression
and a plenitude of affection,
for myself.
I promise,
I would always be tenderly honest,
with myself.
I would know early on that
perfection is paralyzing,
and the beauty in recognizing
how flaws can be strikingly mesmerizing
would take so much pressure,
off of myself.
In my world, gratitude would be the currency
I'd use to acquire my wealth
of compassion and kindness
for others, and most importantly,
for myself.
And for every mistake made,
I would admire the courage in each fall.
For without them, I would be nowhere at all.
And courageously, I would applaud
myself.

In Full Knowing

When I realize that a single honest moment

weighs more than a lifetime of pretending,

I ask myself:

Am I being self-serving or

am I healing wounds,

past and future,

by walking, in full knowing,

toward what burns

and daring to call it home?

Rejections

We posture ourselves away from rejections,

only to realize,

they are simply adjustments

bringing about proper

body, mind, and soul alignment.

The Spaces Between

I am a galaxy,
a thousand pieces of sky spread thin,
trying to figure out where I end
and where the world begins.
They say we're supposed to know
who we are by now,
but I've spent too many nights
wondering how
and why my own reflection
feels like somebody else's creation.
All these strangers look like they know where they're going,
with no direction on a phone's display,
while I'm drawing the map on my palm,
hoping the ink doesn't fade before I find my way.
The tension between the person I am
and the person others want me to be,
of having everything figured out
before I've even had time to breathe.
The moments when identity is in flux,
and the world feels both thrilling and daunting,
I try to balance dreams with reality,
only to stir up more emotional turbulence.
Finally, I grant myself grace to live
in the spaces between questions and answers,
between who I was and who I will be,
and this grace alone sets me free.

Brick by Brick

Are they building love or just performing closeness?
They lie there, breathless and raw,
in the throes of intimacy,
where time slips
and only feeling remains.
In this moment, they are the past,
the present, and the future.
In this moment, unclothed is not naked enough
for the way their souls crave each other.
They engage in love actively and fully,
as a survival instinct,
with drive and relentless intention,
with purpose and a rapacious appetite.
They are lost and unreachable,
captured in the space between dream and reality,
alchemizing the world through vulnerability and touch.
When others are holding hands loosely
and love feels negotiable,
like a force-signed contract with multiple clauses,
they're building love, brick by brick,
patched with mistakes, messy,
but honest and solidly true.

POET MUSE

Off Balance

I thought I was graceful
until I stumbled
when you brushed against me
and faltered
as you pulled me in.
I thought I was graceful
until I fell
into your lap,
and for you.
Was it chemistry
or was it vertigo?
Love doesn't seem to catch you softly.
It is less about grace
and more about how beautifully
you fall.

Heartbreakingly Human

I read about sin,
as if it were a map
to someplace I already know.
Not as a path to damnation,
but as a metaphorical plunge into cold water,
reminding me of what still burns.
Some realizations arrive dizzy,
like they've spun too long in the sun.
You hear the shadows whisper of trespassing,
their silence full of judgment,
but they forget the softness
with which we sometimes cross a line,
not from malice or defiance,
but from a need to connect deeply.
They forget how desire
can feel like devotion,
like healing wrapped neatly in a bow.
And maybe that's the real story,
not of failing,
but of being heartbreakingly human.

Missing From Me

It's not that I miss you.

It's that you are missing from me.

In that sunken area between the heart and the breastbone,

the vital organ not listed,

where the emptiness stabs into flesh

more harshly than a pointed end of a broken bone.

Oh, why am I not made of stone.

This rupture is oozing.

And to remedy the sharp pain, the swelling, and bruising

I keep looking for you

in the 366th day of the year,

eighth day of the week,

25th hour,

61st second.

All in vain.

Perhaps, I lost you in the fifth season.

Will you tell me the reason?

Actually, don't.

I rhyme best when in pain.

Maestro

Make music to my body
with the same neediness
as when you pretend-play piano
upon hearing your favorite melody.
Touch harmony back into my skin
with your usual flair and aplomb.
Tap passionately into my energy, maestro,
leaving me spellbound
by your body mechanics once again.

Phenomenon

My rational thoughts have disappeared
under mysterious circumstances,
like the strange phenomena
observed in the Bermuda Triangle.
The geometry of your shoulders,
your tongue's gentle swirl,
hauled me into this hazardous place,
this realm of no return.
And it wouldn't be a concern,
had the rest of the world
not completely lost me to you.
Had you not felt the need
to wreck another ship.
Had you not reached
for a new trinket
while this one was still sinking,
gasping for air.
How do I swim out of this abyss?
How do I, after my draining endeavor
to rise above nature,
forsake the lover-turned-stranger
in order to set myself free.
Instead,
I keep aching over you
being a thousand kisses
away from me.

Cupid's Error

No one is entirely immune to Cupid's arrow.

The self-proclaimed ice queen has been finally struck,

he did not spare her.

It is the end of an era.

Vulnerability no longer gives rise to terror.

The igloo caging her chest melts,

breaths shift to deep from shallow.

However,

only temporarily,

not forever.

Despite it being a sincere endeavor,

an empath fell in love with a narcissist,

and down her cheeks goes her mascara.

Turns out,

Cupid's arrow

was shot in a terrible error.

Preordained

There's a map between us no one else can read,

a deep understanding that connects our paths.

Every step toward each other feels rehearsed by time.

Every touch feels like a sentence

from the same story we are both dreaming.

We fantasize the same fantasies,

share a mutual longing to escape reality

into the same imagined world,

where our skin speaks in whispers

only we understand.

Our bodies have always known this rhythm,

a deep, steady thrum-thrum

echoing in the pulse of our unmitigated connection.

Déjà vu made flesh

preordained in another moment,

carried from another lifetime.

We're making memories

unbound by past or future.

We are bending time to our will,

walking barefoot on broken clocks.

Softness

I am Winter.

I am cold, often bad-tempered,

unnecessarily harsh,

but secretly gentle.

She is Spring.

By nature, she can melt heavy snowdrifts

that underneath hide a numb heart.

Her lyrical touch lulls my heart

into the most peaceful daydream imaginable,

where I can foresee the inevitable:

a delicate flower grows roots inside a rock.

And paper beats rock for a reason.

With each passing season

she sprouts more flowers around my collarbones.

Now, I am never alone.

She is proof

that open heart prevails over aloof,

sensitive over ruthless,

warm over cold,

because softness is bold.

Softness is Spring,

and my Spring gives me wings.

Lowercase Love

Lowercase love never makes a scene,
she just slips in through the side door
and sits quietly in the corner,
waiting to be noticed.
She doesn't ask for declarations,
only for time and attention,
the space between words where silence hums softly.
She does not shout to be heard.
She trusts she will be understood.
Lowercase love isn't perfect,
but she is constant,
showing up in ways
that don't need capital letters to be real.
She lives in the coffee machine you buy me,
your way of saying, without saying it,

"you deserve a good start."
In the gentle hand squeeze during a tough moment,
or the text that just says "Home?"
Lowercase love is unpretentious,
humble and stripped of performance.
She acknowledges flaws, miscommunication,
the messiness of human connection,
but she always stays.
Some days, I forget she is there.
Other days, I think she has left.
But then I hear her again,
not with volume, but with gravity,
knocking thunderously and sacredly,
reminding me that she never left at all.

Soar

With my breath caught in my throat,

am I drowning or staying afloat?

Unconscious thoughts seep into conversation

at the slightest provocation.

We tease each other's willpower.

You insist,

"One cannot be a hero without first being a coward."

I overcome all my fears completely,

and your warmth melts into me deeply.

Reality blurs into fantasy and vice versa.

Our vital organs are bursting.

A raging inferno overtakes my core.

You're teaching me that I don't need planes to soar.

I Drown

What we are is a slow-burn impulse
stitched into the skin of time,
where surrender is power because it is chosen.
No guard, no filter, just unrelenting presence.
What unravels me is the unspoken fluency
in the way we touch,
a sensual, playful tension stretched across the day,
a slow game of restraint
played in glances and nearness,
a gradual undoing
stripped to emotional nakedness,
as if pulled under by something deep and certain,
a soft submersion into everything I can't name,
until every part of me dissolves into you.
You come in waves,
and I drown willingly.

Home

My home is not in an opulent entrance,
sophisticated crown moldings or grand staircase.
My home is not in a flawlessly made up bed.
It's in the way your chest is carved
perfectly to cushion my head.
My home is not in expensive dishes.
It's in the way you unravel my inhibitions.
My home is not in a prestigious address.
It's in the way you can't help but slip
your hand under my dress.
My home is not in displaying designer baggage.
It's in our inside jokes and secret language.
My home is not in constantly sunny weather.
It's in the way we are never not laughing together.
My home is not in the custom-made window panes.
It's in the silliness of our pet names.
My home is not in a list of guests too long to remember.
It's in how desperate we are for each other's forever.

Faith

It is easier, perhaps, to believe in God
than to question His existence.
I've resisted reverence all my life.
Never pictured myself kneeling in prayer,
until you gave me the most divine feeling.
Now, as I'm on my knees before you,
eyes bowed in quiet devotion,
butterflies stirring my core,
in this sacred act of worship,
I find myself
agnostic no more.

Worth It

I want to spend my love on you,

but these sparks are burning my lungs.

In this battle of tongues,

smiles against mouths,

vows against hours,

my gloss staining your lips,

your stubbornness drowns,

and all you hear are unrestrained

insatiable vowels.

True love always demands poor timing,

Madness tattooed over your heart,

my failed rhyming.

This love story is written in cement.

I am lovesick.

I am love-spent.

Ears bleed from the tearing sensation in my aorta,

but the havoc our farewell wreaked on my being

 was worth it.

Life After Death

There is still life after emotional death for you,

if you've ever inspired a poet.

Engraved in their verses,

praised in their musings,

immortalized in their rhymes.

Proof that nothing we give is ever truly lost,

it only finds new ways to breathe.

Love Multiplies

I am musing on a mental photograph I took

of our ravenous last night.

It's hard to sum everything meaningful

in a soundbite,

so I put pen to paper,

postpone life until later,

relive those moments through cursive

and despite being nervous,

I dedicate to you these verses.

Bed, hair, and thoughts disheveled.

Connection to real life severed.

We're blossoming in each other's arms.

My hands pressed on the wall by your palms.

You outline a heart on my cheek with the tip of your nose.

Your feelings exposed.

And in this life of uncertainty,

with this feeling of urgency,

in this moment,

right this second,

we can see in each other's eyes

how our love multiplies.

Turbulent

Absentmindedly wandering
down memory lane
in search of 'Me-before-You,'
but, luckily, to no avail.
The smooth sailing of your thumb
across my bottom lip
washes away all of my reservations,
and all of a sudden, I want you
to make my calm waters turbulent.

My First

You were my first.

No, not the kiss.

You were my first lost-in-the-moment bliss.

No, not my first crush.

But the swirl of your tongue was the cause

of this everlasting adrenaline rush.

No, not the first to throb at the sight of my curves.

You were the first to give pulse to my words.

No, not my first fantasy.

But the reason I've experienced ecstasy.

No, not my first love.

But when my heart smiles,

you are the only one I think of.

Love Economics

Imagine a world where love is traded like wealth,
where affection is measured in emotional currency,
where devotion becomes urgency,
if you wish to command social worth
and accumulate love credits.
Intimacy is tracked in ledgers,
banks of affection monopolize relationships,
offering loans of temporary warmth at high interest rates.
The emotionally bankrupt resort to "black markets"
of touch and companionship,
where desperation meets exploitation.
The affluent invest in curated relationships.
What if emotional debt goes unpaid?
Does it sound familiar?
Perhaps the world waits for us to rebel,
to fight to make love priceless again,
to break free from a transactional system of closeness,
to prioritize vulnerability over performance,
to break the cycle of calculation,
to choose depth and build slow connections,
to offer our hearts, untainted by economics.

Inspiration

I am overcome with tender pity and sadness

for that girl right across my table.

While I'm enjoying the most decadent breakfast,

her empty eyes are glued to her phone

aimlessly scrolling through content by authors unknown.

I wish she had known

she had just missed the sunrays dancing

across her toast,

and that her artfully served coffee roasts

are now tasteless and cold.

Just like her world.

My world.

Our world.

The one that commodified our likes and dislikes,

and things once seen as unique

are now viewed as standardized.

Knowledge, skill, culture, experience

are now all dispensable.

What a shame. What a spectacle.

We ought to *re*learn the rules of in-person conversation.

We ought to *un*learn this addiction to digital stimulation.

Technology feeds us vain promises and illusory treats.

Oh, how unkempt our internal landscape must be.

Let's tidy it up

by weeding out the need for computerized validation.

For scrolling and clicking

is certainly not how you nurture inspiration.

Love or Lust

Tender is the way to handle
this delicate treasure
whose delicious lingering flavor
turned my bleakness to pleasure,
whose fine aftertaste cannot be erased.
Her.
The one who aroused
an incandescent yearning for more.
The one who made me question
reality under my feet and up above.
How do I know if what I feel is
scorching lust
or counterintuitive love?

Panacea

His mighty hands coalesce
so seamlessly with my delicate skin.
I can sense the panacea for my happiness
at the tips of his fingers.
He went to war against my fears,
annihilating them with his love.
I may have raised the white flag
in surrender and submission,
but by no means was it defeat.

The Poem We Live

Life is like a poem.
It finds meaning in moments, not minutes.
It doesn't need to be long to leave something behind.
So dance when the music finds you,
kiss like it's the first time,
dare a little more than feels safe.
Feel tired only when the day
has wrung out every drop
of your creativity, your joy,
your love, and your desire.

Birth Day

Another revolution around the sun.

Someone told me they wished

they could see the world through my eyes.

And when I asked, "Why?"

they said they'd never felt

a connection to life more potent

after I insisted they search for heaven in every dull moment.

After all, your holy abode lies in the here and now,

in all the fragments and glimpses,

in all the hits and misses,

in all the smiles, frown lines, and freckles,

in every sky that is star-speckled.

Even the empty hellos and painful goodbyes

are simply moments to be poeticized.

I made someone wish

they could see the world through my eyes.

The wish I made each time

I blew out a birthday candle

has been finally realized.

Happily Ever After

I don't have a dream destination,

rather, a dream path.

My life's aftermath

isn't a worry,

even when I'm recklessly tiptoeing

on the thin line between rational and impulsive,

calm and explosive,

when I choose to live life in big doses,

when I don't live by default,

but on purpose.

When I don't seek truths in others,

for they are not found in friends or lovers,

but in your gut,

the world's eighth wonder.

On my dream path,

I don't put my curiosity to rest.

I take chances.

I enjoy conversations with no real answers.

To find magic in the tingling of your fingertips

through the tears and the laughter

is my kind of *happily ever after.*

Take the Lid Off

There is a terror inside me,
shaped like a blank page.
What if I've already said everything that mattered?
Each morning, I wake
and bring my fingers to the keyboard,
wondering if the river has run dry overnight.
Have I become poor in emotional
texture and poetic tension?
In perfect timing, the inner voice of surrender
swollen with inspiration,
exhales from the deepest recesses of my being,
presses its cheek to mine, and whispers:
"Take the lid off. Let your soul spill."
I do as I'm told,
blurring the line between memory and fantasy,
and a new poem pours out,
barefoot and burning.

What We Leave Behind

She just wanted to leave them
with a little more than what they had
when they first met her:
more feelings, more purpose, more poetry.
Silken words and tender moments,
meant to last a lifetime.
But most importantly,
she hoped they would fall in love with themselves,
so they would never know the sting of unrequited love.

Poet Muse

I am both the poet and the muse,

cloaked in daydream and starlight,

a whisper between pages,

a shadow in the margins.

I exist in gentle presence and imagination,

not bound by the hands of time,

but by the depth of thought and emotion.

What I want is to make art

that lingers long after I'm gone,

faceless but felt.

What I want is to help others

see colors more vividly,

feel moments more deeply,

plant a verse in someone's chest to bloom.

I do not hope for recognition.

In fact, I shun it.

Not out of fear,

but out of reverence for the work,

for the mystery.

I write my poems as a gift,

with no return address.

ACKNOWLEDGEMENTS

To you, the reader, thank you for taking this journey with me. These poems are not just words on pages; they are the raw reflections of my heart, my thoughts, and my experiences. I hope that within these lines, you find pieces of yourself, perhaps fragments you never knew existed or emotions you thought were uniquely yours.

To my daughter, you are the muse who drives me to explore, express, and dream. Every accomplishment I pursue is fueled by the strength and purpose you bring into my life. I hope one day you see the beauty in these words and feel the boundless love and admiration I hold for you.

To my husband, thank you for standing beside me through every draft, doubt, and dream. Your encouragement and constant belief have carried me further than you know.

To my parents, thank you for always holding me in the highest regard, for believing in me before I believed in myself, and for instilling in me the confidence to pursue my passions with courage and heart.

To my best friend, your support is my foundation, your love is my constant. Thank you for making me feel seen, heard, and deeply understood. You give me the courage to be all I am.

To the Thought Catalog Books team, thank you for believing in my voice and giving my words a home. Your support and care helped shape this collection into what it was meant to be. And thank you to Allie Michelle, whose big heart and generosity connected us. Your kindness continues to inspire.

ABOUT THE AUTHOR

Sasha Nudél, a poet, speech-language pathologist, and certified fitness trainer born in Ukraine, is passionate about exploring the intricacies of human experience. Her poetry delves into love, sensuality, and the lust for life, capturing the raw beauty of connection and desire. With a distinctive voice and deep understanding of the human condition, Sasha invites readers on a transformative journey of emotion and intimacy. Her work celebrates the complexities of passion, longing, and vulnerability.

Now based between New Jersey and New York, Sasha continues to share her poetry with a growing audience. Follow her journey on Instagram @sashanudel.

REFLECTION PAGES

Dear Reader, this space is yours.
Fill it with your thoughts, reflections, and
the poetry that emerges from within.
It's your turn to create, reflect, and discover yourself.

MORE FROM
THOUGHT CATALOG BOOKS

And Yet—Here You Are
Eileen Lamb

It Is All Equally Fragile
Alison Malee

The Art Of Who We Are
Robert W. Dean

The Gods We Made
Blake Auden

Emotional Aesthetics
Ashley Klassen

The Words We Left Behind
Callie Byrnes

Moments To Hold Close
Molly Burford

Face Yourself. Look Within.
Adrian Michael

The Pivot Year
Brianna Wiest

THOUGHT
CATALOG
Books

THOUGHTCATALOG.COM